Lightbulb Moments

UNPLANNED LESSONS FOR TEACHERS FROM TEACHERS

GAIL BOUSHEY   **ALLISON BEHNE**

ISBN:978-1-61892-010-2
Cover design by Madeline Boushey
Typesetting by Dusty Embree

Contributors

Kristin Ackerman
Ellen Greany
Melissa McNally
Trish Prentice
Lori Sabo
Laura Secrist

Dedicated to teachers everywhere.

You spark curiosity in your students that fuels their love of learning.

What *you* do makes a difference.

Contents

Introduction

We find a lesson hidden in almost every story of daily life. When we take time to reflect on these stories and make a connection that inspires us, we call it a lightbulb moment. It is the aha moment when we are called to action or reminded of our purpose.

That is what this book is made of. It contains 50 short stories from everyday life that turned into lightbulb moments for us as educators. Each story is accompanied by a quote and then an area where you can make notes about what speaks to you.

The teaching profession faces a barrage of demands and changes every year, from new students to curriculum changes—and now, even location shifts. (Are you working virtually, in person, in a hybrid setting, or do you even know this week!?). As educators, we adjust and move forward in the best interest of our students. We expect change. It is inevitable. And, we can't forget to take care of ourselves. We need time to de-stress. Time to reflect, be inspired, and refocus our energy.

Of course, we wish this book could take care of all that! We wish you could read this book and all of your work stress would lift and all happiness and normalcy would return. But we know that nothing short of a miracle will make that happen instantly. However, we do think this book can help. Whether before, during, or after school, set aside five to 10 minutes for yourself. Grab your favorite beverage, read one short story, and reflect on how it relates to your experience. That's it! Just you, your book, and your thoughts.

Reflection is the key to growth and learning. It "gives the brain an opportunity to pause amidst the chaos, untangle and sort through observations and experiences, consider multiple possible interpretations, and create meaning. This meaning becomes learning, which can then inform future mindsets and actions" (Porter, 2017). Reflection can help reduce stress and enhance happiness.

This book is not meant to be read all in one sitting, but in small increments. Pick it up (it's not heavy), choose a story (in any order—we won't tell you what to read first), mark it up with your thoughts (we've provided space for you), and then let it inspire you to look for lightbulb moments in your everyday life (they're there, we promise). As you are purposeful in your reflection, you will find that these moments are everywhere. We spend a lot of time and energy planning our days with students, and yet these little moments, these "lightbulb moments," are unplanned lessons that inspire and refocus us, day in and day out.

Gail & Allison

Time to put the plan book away and turn the lights on . . .

Reference: Porter, J. (2017). Why you should make time for self-reflection (even if you hate doing it). *Harvard Business Review.* Retrieved from https://hbr.org/2017/03/why-you-should-make-time-for-self-reflection-even-if-you-hate-doing-it

Teaching Is My Passion

In all of my teaching, I think about what I find fascinating and what I would love to learn more about. I use my teaching to grow, and that makes me, even after all these years, a fresh and eager teacher. — Carol Dweck

I was reflecting with a group of teachers when one of them said, "Teaching is my passion. Getting better is my job." The words stopped me in my tracks. When I asked her to repeat them, she said again, "Teaching is my passion. Getting better is my job." The quote is now recorded in my journal, where it stares me down, daring me to make it my own.

Most of us are passionate about being teachers. We care deeply about helping all students achieve high levels of success as well as helping them become kind and productive citizens. It is this passion that leads us to increase our knowledge and hone our skills, becoming the best teachers  we can be. Carol Dweck says, "You recognize that the growth of your skills is in your hands, and you choose to make that happen" (Dweck, 2014).

How do we get better at our jobs? How do we take the

growth of our own skills into our hands?

- By gaining ideas and techniques from professional literature
- By observing outstanding teachers in action in their rooms and in professional development settings
- By participating in candid conversations with colleagues
- By setting professional goals, and then taking action in incremental steps that will enable us to achieve them
- By taking advantage of technology: watching teaching videos, following teaching blogs, interacting on teacher Twitter chats, and more

Having passion is just part of the equation of being a good teacher. Getting better at what we do is what will make the greatest difference for the students we serve.

We've already got the passion. Let's continue to refine our skills and bring greatness to our craft.

Gail Boushey

Dweck, C. (2014). Teachers' mindsets: "Every Student has Something to Teach Me" *Educational Horizons, 93*(2), 10–15. https://doi.org/10.1177/0013175X14561420

 What speaks to me . . .

Be A Carrier

A healthy attitude is contagious but don't wait to catch it from others. Be a carrier. — Tom Stoppard

On my way home from a teaching conference in Pennsylvania, my flight was delayed because of fog. When I heard we had a 30-minute delay, my initial response was

disappointment mixed with relief that I didn't have to worry about a connecting flight. However, those around me had feelings that were a bit stronger:

"This is ridiculous! I have places to be!"
"Here we go again . . . The airline couldn't care less that I have a deadline to make."

"So this ruins my whole day!"

The attendant and pilot kept us updated every 10 to 15 minutes, added a sincere apology with each announcement, and tended to disgruntled customers in between. The woman next to me started a conversation about how we should go up and demand travel vouchers for the inconvenience. A gentleman in the group very respectfully interjected that he was thankful for the delay. He said he felt fortunate to live in a day and age where they have the technology to know flying conditions and keep passengers safe. He explained, "Do you want them flying with less than a quarter mile visibility? I don't."

It was his attitude and courage to speak up that created a ripple effect in the crowd and silenced grumbles.

This made me think of the quote by Tom Stoppard, "A healthy attitude is contagious but don't wait to catch it from others. Be a carrier." This applies in our daily lives.

Regardless of the role we play—teacher, parent, colleague, leader, or learner—our attitude influences others. Let's make a concerted effort to use the opportunities to be carriers of kindness, thoughtfulness, and respect, so our ripple effect is a positive one.

Allison Behne

 What speaks to me . . .

You Tell Me

The important thing is not to stop questioning. Curiosity has its own reason for existing. — Albert Einstein

At two and a half years old, our granddaughter Hadley is asking a lot of questions. "Why is it raining? Why is my brother crying? What are you doing?" Answering Hadley's questions requires a lot of thought on our part, and we often find ourselves asking questions of her in return. Lately, when we ask Hadley questions, she responds with "You tell me" and waits until she can agree with our response.

"Hadley, who did you see today?"
"You tell me."

"Hadley, where did you go today?"
"You tell me."

"Hadley, what did you play today?"
"You tell me."

It is fascinating to hear Hadley turn our questions back to us, as if she doesn't see any reason to give us an answer that we already know. How often does this happen in our classes, especially with students who may be a little more school savvy? We have students who are willing to play the game of answering these lower-order questions, even when they know we already know the answer. We can do better.

Questions can be categorized in many different ways—

from Bloom's taxonomy to Ted Wragg's empirical, conceptual, and value questions, to Taffy Rafael's Question Answer Relationship. However, all of these approaches include a basic differentiation between lower-order and higher-order questions. Lower-order questions usually start with who, what, when, or where. Relying on basic recall, children can answer such questions with a single right answer. In contrast, higher-order questions, which may begin with how, why, and which, are important because they require children to think on a deeper level.

Teachers ask between three and four hundred questions each day, well over 60 percent of which fall into the lower-order category. Many of our questions are organizational tools used to check the completion of work, summarize what has been taught, and evaluate whether learning has occurred. Our higher-level questions have the added potential to motivate, develop thinking skills, and enhance knowledge. Strategies such as familiarizing ourselves with the different levels of questions, writing down a few "go-to" higher-order questions, and adding wait time when we ask them have considerable promise for improving classroom instruction and student learning.

From now on, I am going to take a note from Hadley and ask "Why?" more often—and then wait for a response.

Gail Boushey

 What speaks to me . . .

Pause, Be Present, Smile

Wherever you are, be all there. — Jim Elliot

You know those days when you have a million things to do and barely enough time to do them? The school year is filled with activities—school programs, sports events, conferences, report cards, assessments, holidays . . . and the list goes on. It was on a day like this a few years ago that I learned a valuable lesson.

Let me start by setting the stage: I had worked a full day, report cards were due, I had two birthdays to shop for (including a party that started in 30 minutes), it was parent watch night at my daughter's dance class, and I had a sick husband at home.

As I hurried into a sporting goods store with my seven-year-old son, Nathan, to buy a birthday gift, he was jabbering away. A minute later, however, I suddenly

realized that I couldn't see or hear him. I yelled his name and looked all around the store, but I couldn't find him. Then I noticed that one mannequin didn't quite match the rest. There was my son, head tucked inside his shirt . . . frozen. At first, I was not amused. Did he not understand that we were in a hurry? We were going to be late! But just as I opened my mouth to tell him to knock it off, I paused—smiled—and started to laugh. Realizing that this moment should be etched in time, I grabbed my camera and took a photo as we both giggled uncontrollably. Then, together, my son and I laughed our way to the checkout lanes and headed for the party.

I share this story because it's a good reminder that we should always allow ourselves time to pause, be present, and smile. When I came across this photo the other day, I was immediately transported back to that moment in the store a few years ago. I remember clearly how adorable my son looked and the giggles we shared at his harmless silliness. I don't remember what we purchased as a gift or whether we made it to the party on time. But I will never forget the fun and laughter of that bright spot in the middle of a day filled with craziness.

I am guessing that you, too, know how easy it is to get lost inside a busy day. We all have days and even weeks when we think that we just don't have time to slow down and enjoy much of anything. And although many of the things we do are necessary, it is important to remember to pause, be present, and take time to enjoy the moment. Laugh at what's funny, appreciate the small gestures, and smile when something makes you happy. If your students see how important that is to you, they will learn to do the same.

Allison Behne

 What speaks to me . . .

One Size Does Not Fit All

If a child can't learn the way we teach, maybe we should teach the way they learn. — Ignacio Estrada

My husband Joey is a strength and conditioning coach for a Major League Baseball team. People outside professional sports often misunderstand his job and mistake him for an athletic trainer. I explain that whereas athletic trainers provide athletes with treatment to recover from injuries, strength and conditioning coaches provide a training regimen aimed at preventing injuries. Their job is to keep athletes in optimum shape so they can perform at their highest level. It's vitally important that the athletic trainer and the strength and conditioning coach communicate regularly with each other to support their athletes in the best possible way.

At the Major League level, there is no doubt that every athlete is talented. They've worked tirelessly in the minor leagues and proven that they have what it takes to play at this level. However, there is a big difference between the Triple-A, the highest minor league level, and "The Show." In the Major Leagues, the competition becomes even more rigorous. Small, sometimes seemingly insignificant things can make the difference between athletes being good at their sport and being great at their sport. Each athlete is looking for that tweak that will give them the edge over others who are competing for their job.

As I shared about how hard these athletes work and explained the day-to-day routine of Joey's job, I realized that it parallels what we do with our students in many ways. Just as my husband provides all athletes with the same two or three foundational workouts, we provide our students with two or three brief foundational focus lessons. And

just as we provide our students with individualized goals, small-group lessons, and regular conferring sessions (because each child is different), Joey works to provide his athletes with individualized supplemental exercises and workouts (because each athlete is different).

This "aha!" moment reminds me of the importance of relationship building and truly knowing our students as learners. Individualized instruction can target their areas of need and give them an edge towards success.

Think about your current teaching practices – how do you get to know your students as learners? What questions do you ask to dive deeper? How does this information inform your practice?

Ellen Greany

What speaks to me . . .

Lasting Community

The first priority in the classroom, even over learning, should be the teacher student relationship. This relationship far outweighs any other technique created by educators to further a student's academic achievement. — Heather T. Forbes, Help for Billy

The relationship and community we build with students—how to be kind, how to listen, how to speak respectfully—increases academic learning and positively influences relationships. The effects can last far beyond the 180 days we spend together. I recently rediscovered this truth upon reconnecting with Dorothy.

Dorothy and I grew up together and were schoolmates throughout our education. Friendship was built through joint classes, similar interests, and small-town life. I hadn't seen her for 20 years, but when she saw on Facebook that I was at the Pennsylvania Reading Conference, she sent me a private message asking if we could get together and catch up. Since I was leaving the next morning, the only option was to have her pick me up from my hotel at 5:00 a.m. and take me to the airport. She readily agreed to do so.

We were together in the car for one hour. We filled the 60 minutes with talking, listening, and laughing as fast as we could. We teared up a few times, relishing being near enough to see each smile line, dimple, and hand gesture that we had grown to know well so many years ago. After one long-lasting hug, I raced to catch my flight.

Upon landing, I was greeted with this message:

Thanks for such a dynamic start to what have might otherwise been a regular day. How cool is it that we can so easily discuss life's twists and turns, find so much in common even after decades (yikes) have passed, and both be so connected to similar passions like reading and kids and shepherding the growth of colleagues and introvert/extrovert combinations and family dynamics . . . Imagine the ground we could have covered in two hours!
Makes me smile and pause, wonder and ponder about how significantly our earlier life experiences and environments impact us.
-Dorothy

Then   and   Now

As teachers, we build strong relationships with our students, and all the while students are learning to build relationships with each other. The community we weave together, thread by thread, has the potential to stay together for a lifetime, if by chance they run into each other again.

Gail Boushey

What speaks to me . . .

I Don't Know ... Or Do I?

Find the right questions. You don't invent the answers you reveal the answers. — Dr. Jonas Salk

In a recent meeting, a colleague asked me a question that I was unsure how to answer. I thought about it for a moment and then replied, "I don't know." The answer "I don't know" usually prompts the person asking the question to either look for an answer elsewhere or share their own thoughts on the subject. My colleague, however, did not follow either of those paths. Instead, he posed a second question: "If you did know, what would you say?" When he asked this second question, I started to answer immediately—but then I paused, realizing what had just happened. My colleague had pushed me to think through something that I would have been quick to dismiss otherwise. That simple question, as he explained to me with a smile, can reveal significant thoughts when used at the right time. He encouraged me to try it with my students or even with my own children at home.

Here is what I found when I tried this at school:

> One child "didn't know" what 4 plus 3 equals. But she said that if she did know, she would say 7, because 4 plus 4 equals 8 and this was only one less. Another child "didn't know" how to read the word *giraffe*. However, she said that if she did know how to read it, she would say "*giraffe*." Why? Because the picture on the page was of a giraffe, and it made sense in the sentence. And finally, a

third child "didn't know" why it was difficult for her to stay in one spot when reading. When asked what she would say if she did know why, however, she answered that she was able to see what all her friends were doing and wanted to be a part of it.

And at home, here's what happened:

My son didn't know where the pile of things on his floor should go. But if he did know, he would say the sweatshirt went in the laundry hamper, the jeans went in the closet, the baseball cards went in his case, the book belonged on the shelf, and the Kleenex should be tossed in the trash. My daughter didn't know why she had answered so many questions incorrectly on her biology test. If she did know, however, she would say it was probably because she had waited to study until the night before.

I don't know if this probing question will always produce the answers for which I am looking. But if I did know, I would say it is a great tool to promote deeper thinking from our students, colleagues, and even ourselves.

Allison Behne

 What speaks to me . . .

Comfort and Joy

If students are stressed out, information cannot get in. This is a matter of science. — Judy Willis, MD

I remember being in first grade. Sitting in the last seat of the last row, I memorized the back of the head in front of me. The room had a chill about it. It was pin-drop silent, except for the occasional announcement in a voice that reminded me of Charlie Brown's teacher: "Waaa, waaa, waaa, waaaa . . ."

This image is burned into my memory. I didn't like school, which was starkly different from the joyful home I would leave each morning. The contrast created disequilibrium, stress, and anxiety that I didn't know how to navigate. I found it challenging to focus on reading when I wasn't comfortable in my surroundings.

I have spent years—you might even say my whole life— researching and observing the effect of classroom environments on children and the teachers who create those environments. I have often wondered how different my own school years would have been if my teachers had welcomed us at the door. What if my classroom environment had included reading with other students, working in cozy areas filled with pillows and rugs, a happy hum of music and quiet talk, and friendships?

Thankfully we know more now than when I started school. Thanks to brain research, we know that students' comfort level has a profound influence on their brains' ability to process and retain information. When teachers use strategies to reduce stress and build a positive emotional and physical environment, students gain emotional resilience. They learn more efficiently and at higher levels of cognition.

What can you do to create such an environment?

> 1.   Take care of yourself. Replenish, reinvigorate, be happy, and rejoice in who you are as a teacher. Remind yourself that you are the best YOU there is!

> 2.   Create joy in your life and exude that joy to others. Joy and enthusiasm are absolutely essential for learning to take place in adults and children. See the joy that is all around us—and if you don't see it, create it for yourself and others. Carry joy with you always.

> 3.   Bring joy into your classroom through words and actions. Enjoy the beautiful learning environment you have created—from the smiles with which you greet your students to your one-on-one conferring to celebrate each student's progress toward becoming the very best they can be.

We are responsible for creating environments in our rooms that allow and encourage students to thrive and excel. We can and should invite them into environments that help them reach their full potential while immersed in joy.

Gail Boushey

 What speaks to me . . .

Inspired, Informed, Empowered

I want to inspire people. I want someone to look at me and say,
"Because of you, I didn't give up." — Unknown

A few weeks ago, our neighbors invited us to a coach's
clinic, where guest speakers would be talking about
strength training. Although I wasn't overly excited about
the opportunity, my son and husband were looking
forward to it, so the night of the clinic I decided to go,
smile, and make the most of it. Little did I know that I
would end up enjoying the evening as much as, if not more
than, my husband and son. There were a handful of
speakers that evening, but two of them had advice of value
for coaches and teachers.

The first speaker of the evening, Rob Stock, a former
Navy Seal, is with Human Performance Initiative, training
athletes. He spoke about how an individual's attitude and
outlook directly changes everything around him. Using his
experience as a Navy Seal and the story of his recovery
from a horrendous injury received while at war, he inspired
coaches to instill in their athletes how important attitude is
to success. His message was well received by the coaches
present, but also by me as a teacher. My attitude and
outlook affect the attitude and outlook of my colleagues,
parents, and students. I have the power to help move them
forward or delay their success by the impressions I leave.

Chris Carlisle, former strength coach for the Seattle
Seahawks, was the final speaker of the evening, and was he
ever passionate about his profession! He began by telling

coaches he was not there to tell them what to do because he said, "If you do what I do, you will fail miserably!"

He went on to talk about how every team is different and that to really be effective, coaches need to know the game and know their players. His advice, which is great advice for teachers as well, was this:

- Deconstruct the game . . .Tear it apart to its deepest element.
- Get out of the box and do something different. If what you are doing isn't working, ask yourself why, and change something.
- Ask why! Read and become educated about your profession so that when you make decisions, they are based on what you decided and not what someone else told you to do.
- Establish a knowledge bank. Find people who know and are the best at what they do. Learn from them.
- Be dynamic. Make small changes. Wake up and do one thing different . . .Work with that one thing, and when it soaks in, change one more thing. That is how you become great.

I left that evening inspired to make a difference, informed with ways to make change happen, and empowered by my ability to do so.

Allison Behne

 What speaks to me . . .

The Mary Poppins Principle

What we learn with pleasure, we never forget.
— Alfred Mercier

Here is the description of the water aerobics class I like to attend: "Get fit with this challenging water workout! Improve strength and cardiovascular endurance without the impact on your joints. Burn up to 400 calories." I have participated during different days and hours under the tutelage of five different instructors. They all knew the content. They used similar teaching strategies and curriculum. Yet one stands above all the others so much that I now look at the calendar to make sure she is teaching before I don my dreaded swimsuit and make myself go.

The difference? She makes it fun. People who attend her class want to be there. We enjoy our time together. We work hard and rarely glance at the clock to see how much time is left. It is obvious that she enjoys what she is doing. Her attitude and energy are contagious, causing us to enjoy what we are doing as well.

I can't help but think about how this might relate in our classrooms. We have district, state, and even national standards to meet. We have resources we must use. But if we really love being there every day, love the students we've been blessed with, and are passionate about the content and the benefits of what we are imparting, they can't help but love being there, too.

We laugh often in my classroom. We infuse fun whenever possible, whether it's pretending to be ninjas as we move down the hall, or playing Mrs. Sabo Says during brief transitions. When it's time to clean up at the end of  the day, we do it to music, ending with a brief dance party before settling down for one last story or poem.

Many years ago, Bob Sherman wrote a song for *Mary Poppins* that has become my fun mantra for life. Do you remember how "A Spoonful of Sugar" starts?

> In ev'ry job that must be done
> There is an element of fun
> You find the fun and snap!
> The job's a game.

I'm not naive enough to think that everything we do is going to be fun, especially when hard work is involved. But I think there is a principle here worth internalizing. A spirit of fun is valuable and infectious. If it improves motivation and engagement for our students, like it does for my friends and me at the gym, it's worth getting our fun on!

Lori Sabo

 What speaks to me . . .

The Sounds of Quiet

Progress is rarely silent, now go make some noise today.
— Unknown

I have been getting up really early lately. I love mornings and the quiet that seems so productive and promising. When our house is devoid of voices and activity in the early hours, it seems silent at first. Yet when I tune in, my ears perceive a layer of sound previously unnoticed: the song of a robin outside, a distant car engine, the creak of a floorboard, and the gentle whirring of my computer. These sounds are not intrusive but serve as a gentle backdrop, and I find that my thoughts are clear and focused, and that I am able to accomplish a lot.

I am reminded that quiet doesn't mean silent, at home or in our classrooms. When I first started teaching, I thought the room had to be silent to be productive. I now know that just like productive struggle is good, productive noise is, too. This is why a gentle hum can be a good thing. Students may be saying a word aloud as they break it apart in an attempt to spell it correctly. They may be laughing or gasping at a text that caused an emotional response. Or a Read to Someone partner may be softly asking, "Do you want coaching or time?"

So now, before I am tempted to remind students to be quiet, I pay close attention. If I discover it is simply the hum of engagement, I take a breath, smile, and get back to the small group or conference at hand, enjoying the sounds of quiet.

Gail Boushey

 What speaks to me . . .

The Serving Spoon

The difference between ordinary and extraordinary is that little extra. — Jimmy Johnson

When I was growing up, we went to my grandma's house every Sunday for lunch. I always looked forward to it because we'd be surrounded by grandparents, aunts, uncles, and cousins. Another highlight was Grandma's home-cooked meals. She was an amazing cook! The only thing I didn't like were the vegetables that ended up on my plate each Sunday. They were always the last thing left, staring me down, preventing my departure from the table.

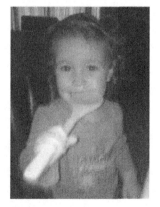

Fortunately for me, in addition to being a good cook, my grandma was a good problem solver. She offered me a large serving spoon and said I could eat my vegetables with the big spoon if I wanted. It was a novelty, something different, and worked like a charm. Those unappetizing vegetables tasted better on the big spoon than they did on my regular spoon.

My grandma took something I viewed as unpleasant and made it not only doable, but enjoyable. By simply changing one small thing, she altered my view and did so without a struggle. Wouldn't it be great if we could do the same for our students?

Each day, we teach a room full of students with varying personalities and abilities. Some love to read. Others love math. Some students are there solely for the social aspects school has to offer. Yet we must teach reading to children who don't like to read, math to children who don't like math, and independent learning skills to children who prefer to socialize. This is not a simple task, but I do believe it is possible.

Reflecting on what I learned from my grandma, I realize I need to look for the "serving spoon" that will inspire my students to digest the unpalatable. Maybe it's providing choice over the books they read, the place they sit, or the order in which they engage in reading and writing practice. Perhaps it's providing opportunities to share at the end of the day, time to read with a buddy, or the privilege of using a special bookmark. Possibly it will be through the empowerment they feel after learning a new reading strategy. I may not find their "serving spoon" on the first try, or even the second, but if I keep trying, I know I'll find it. I encourage you to do the same.

Allison Behne

 What speaks to me . . .

Where Will Your Travels Take You?

Alone we can do so little; together we can do so much.
— Helen Keller

Anne Plenkovich and Gail

This photo was taken in Dubai . . . all because of one teacher and a positive collegial relationship that developed when we worked together, a relationship that continued to grow even after we moved to different districts, states, countries, and continents.

Building relationships with students and colleagues is one of the highlights of our career. We spend hours each day with our students. We may spend more time with our colleagues than we do with our own families, laughing at lunch, learning together, nudging one another professionally, poring over data, and reflecting on student successes and challenges. It is no wonder so many of them become lifelong friends.

I've joined many of my teaching friends on journeys: traveling to each other's classrooms so we can plan together as a team, congregating to discuss and learn from professional books, and relying on and supporting each other through challenges that come our way, all the while learning more about each other and deepening our friendship.

Whether you travel down the hall, through the Internet, or around the world, students benefit from the thinking, conversations, and learning that we do together. Where will you travel today?

Gail Boushey

 What speaks to me . . .

Simply Amazing

You are capable of amazing things.
— Unknown

A corporate comedy magician was the evening's entertainment at my husband's holiday party. As soon as I heard this, my plan was to sit in the back and hide, as I am not a person who likes to volunteer in events like this. Not only do I try to disappear in the crowd, but I often miss much of the event because I spend so much time worrying about being called on. How silly is that? I am an outgoing individual and have no problem speaking in front of others, yet when put on the spot, I freeze. I am happy to say, I made it through the evening without being noticed, and I learned a thing or two in the process.

The first thing I learned was that worrying about something can make an activity much less enjoyable. I did enjoy my evening, but I didn't enjoy it as much as I would have without the consuming worry of being called on. This makes me reflect on my teaching. Do my students fear being called on? Are they getting as much out of my class as they should be? How can I create an atmosphere where my students can relax and enjoy their learning process?

The second thing I learned came from the magician himself. During his performance, he spoke about the mystery of magic. He said one of the great things about magic is that it can take something simple and make it amazing. A deck of cards is simple, but when combined with a magic trick, it becomes amazing. He referred to various professions that can turn simple into amazing. A painter can take a simple piece of paper and a jar of paint and turn it into an amazing piece of art. A musician can take seven simple notes and turn them into an amazing song. A chef can take a few simple ingredients and turn them into an amazing dish.

I continued to reflect on the teaching profession. We go from simple to amazing every day! We help students take simple letters and turn them into amazing words. We teach them to take simple words and make amazing sentences. We teach them that a simple story can become something amazing when we use our vocabulary skills to understand the words and our fluency skills to read with expression. Every day we have the opportunity to take a child's learning from being "required" (simple) to being "amazing" through our enthusiasm and commitment to learning. And truthfully, how amazing is that?

I challenge you to think about your role with students. What is it you do that moves simple to amazing? My guess is you will be pleasantly surprised at how amazing you truly are!

Allison Behne

 What speaks to me . . .

Seasons

If nothing ever changed, there'd be no butterflies.
— Unknown

There is a rhythm to the art of teaching. It's as dependable as the constant change of the seasons themselves. Fall brings the hopeful excitement of a new school year. Pencils with pristine erasers are sharpened and eager to find paper. Books are poised and ready to be shared. Many of them are dog-eared favorites, and some are brand new with stiff pages almost stuck together. Teachers are geared up to make a difference. Children arrive, and it all begins. Relationships are established while routines and expectations are set. Learning is put in motion, and life begins to get very busy. Each day is exciting but hectic, with a never-ending list of tasks to juggle. Just when it all feels like too much; the holiday break arrives and provides a well-deserved respite.

Winter blows in with the promise of new beginnings. Often, this is the most productive time of year. Everyone is glad to be back in a routine. Maturity is beginning to peek out from behind the ears of those children who need it most. Assessments show (for most of our students) that the hard work throughout the fall is paying off. Winter is also a time to think fresh, outside the box. Continuing to do the same thing with that one child will only get the same results. It can be invigorating to get creative and try something new and different. If there's a chance at having a significant effect on the life of a child, take it.

Spring comes with warm breezes and distracted minds. There is a time change, outdoor sports, and of course, the promise of summer. The children know each other well by now. They have brother/sister relationships, including the ability to push buttons for personal entertainment. All of this can make it challenging to keep focused. On the flip side, the last few months of school are an incredibly sweet time. Much has been accomplished and should be joyously celebrated. Savor the one-of-a-kind moments. Relish this particular community so intentionally built because it will never come together quite this way again.

Summer! There are no e-mails, behavior management needs, forms to fill out, meetings to attend, parent conferences, referrals, report cards, fire drills, assemblies, recess duties, or lunch counts. Instead, it's all about you and your teaching! There is time to read a professional book or two to elevate your skills. You can reflect on what works well and what changes you wish to make. There is time to appreciate the joys of your work and refresh for the coming year. Isn't summer wonderful?

The teaching profession is like no other. It is true that much is expected, but much is returned as well. We get a front-row seat from which to watch children learn. Laughter, enthusiasm, and fresh outlooks are perks to enjoy. Each new day is another opportunity to share passion for learning and teaching—a gift, if you choose to open it.

Trish Prentice

 What speaks to me . . .

My Days Are Full, My Life Is Full

Nobody is ever too busy, it's just a matter of priorities.
— Unknown

Have you been busy lately? Have you been crazy busy? Do you think you may be even busier than any of your friends?

I read an article in which the author said that some of us view busyness as a badge of honor and that complaining about it is really boasting in disguise. I will admit there have been times I have tried to one-up a person when they were lamenting their busyness.

We are busy because of the choices we make. Think about the activities you do with your family, the time you spend working with students at school, the phone calls you make to parents after school, the extra errands you run for lessons you are teaching or taking, the exercise you do to stay healthy . . . All of those activities take time, and we are "busy" doing them all.

Maybe we need to change the word *busy* to *full*. Perhaps it is actually a privilege to be able to fill our days with the activities we deem most important.

That simple switch helps us reframe a negative connotation so that it is a positive one. Then we're able to acknowledge how lucky we are to have a life made of days filled with what we choose to do. Let's celebrate and cherish the fullness of our days.

Gail Boushey

What speaks to me . . .

Thank Goodness It's Monday

The greatest discovery of all time is that a person can change his future by merely changing his attitude.
— Oprah Winfrey

I am not a morning person. I never have been, and chances are I never will be. Most mornings when my alarm goes off, I hit the snooze button a few times before I face the reality that I have to get up and get started for the day. Last Friday, however, my alarm went off, and instead of hitting snooze, I turned off my alarm and got up to get ready. I knew that it was the last work day, and I was ready to get started so that my weekend could begin.

Does this sound familiar to you? Even if you are a morning person, is your attitude about getting ready for work slightly different on Friday than it is Monday through Thursday? Have you ever gone to work on a Friday thinking "Woo Hoo! It is Friday! I can make it!" On Friday when you enter the school doors, you are often greeted with smiles and at least one or two colleagues remind you, "TGIF!" as you walk to your classroom. Most Fridays, the aura of a school or workplace is different than it is the other days of the week. It is happier, more upbeat; you see more smiles and feel more energy as you walk through the halls. Why is this? What is it about Friday that can change the atmosphere of a building and the attitudes of those inside?

The same example goes for Monday, only it is the reverse. Think about walking into school on a Monday morning.

Chances are you will be greeted by someone asking if you had a nice weekend, or others telling you the events of their weekend. However, chances are also likely that someone will say, "Is it Friday yet?" Some teachers run around Monday mornings getting last minute things together for their class, and others spend time visiting with their colleagues about what the week holds. Either way, I think many would agree that the atmosphere on Monday is different than on Friday.

Imagine the impact we would have on our students if we had a "Friday attitude" every day of the week?

As educators, our attitude impacts students, colleagues, and parents every day. We don't get the choice to only have school on Fridays. We have school five days a week. We do, however, get to choose the attitude we have on the days we are there. Maybe we should try to go in on a Monday with the "TGIM" attitude and see where that gets us. I have a hunch if all of us went by this, our school atmosphere may be a little more welcoming and the effect of this positive energy on students could only lead to great things.

Allison Behne

 What speaks to me . . .

Holiday Gifts

The meaning of life is to find your gift. The purpose of life is to give it away. — *Pablo Picasso*

Holidays evoke images of gifts, yet the best gifts of all might not be the ones we wrap.

The gifts within you, that you share each and every day, are gifts of lasting worth.

The gift of kindness—
kind action and word.
The gift of time—
to listen and be heard.

The gift of love
shared by look, hug, or smile
warms the heart
and lasts a long while.

The gift of a hand
held out for support
will lift one up
to encourage, transport.

The gift of laughter—
one story, one rhyme—
positively affects
each of us over time.

The gift of respect
and acceptance for all,
of similarities and differences,
valuing them all.

The gift of hope,
bravely radiated today,
opens hearts and minds
to endless possibilities in each day.

Share more of these gifts with those on your list and they
will certainly be received joyously, making our world a
better place.

Gail Boushey

 What speaks to me . . .

The First Day Difference

What is it that makes the first day of school so special? Is it the smell of freshly waxed floors or shampooed carpets? Or the new crayon tips and empty notebooks? It could be the chance to see friends and meet the teacher. The list of first day experiences could go on and on. When my husband and I dropped our son off for his first day of first grade, I was able to see what makes the first day extraordinary. It is the enthusiasm and excitement of students, teachers, school staff, and parents.

When I pulled into the parking lot of my son's school, I could sense the difference. Cars lined the streets, people were friendly, pictures were being taken here and there, and parents and children walked briskly, eager to get in the doors of the school. Inside there were smiles, laughter, and even a few tears (students and parents alike). Teachers stood in the doorways, greeting children with a smile, and children followed directions as curiosity of their new teacher filled their minds. The first day is unlike any other day.

As I left my son at school to begin his first-grade career, I couldn't help but think of what it would be like if students, teachers, staff, and parents kept that enthusiasm all year long. What if parents put the same effort (as they do on the first day) into preparing their children for school each day? What if students worked to make a positive impression on their teacher by modelling "first-day behavior" year-round? What if school staff were as friendly and helpful to students and parents daily? And, what if teachers not only greeted students at the door each morning, but they also had the positive energy and engagement they display in the first week?

I know it cannot be done alone, but we can do our part. As your year begins, think about what it is that makes the first day so special for you and your students. What can you do to help your students, their parents, and your co-workers keep their "first-day enthusiasm"?

Take a picture of your class on the first day. (Don't forget to include yourself in the picture!) Then, post this picture in your plan book, on the class wall, in a frame on your desk, or anywhere else you see fit. Use this picture as an "in your face" reminder of how eager and enthusiastic your students (and you) were on the first day, and as a motivator to keep it going. Remember, the back-to-school smells, supplies, and friends are important, but it is the enthusiasm and excitement that truly makes the difference.

Allison Behne

 What speaks to me . . .

Pivot!

A pivot is a change in strategy without a change in vision.
— Eric Ries

If you are a fan of the TV show Friends, you are most likely familiar with the episode where Ross buys a brand-new couch. To get the couch up to his apartment, it has to go up flights of stairs. Ross, Chandler, and Rachel carry the oversized couch up the too-narrow stairwell, turning it as Ross yells, "Pivot!" over and over in an effort to make it fit.

P·I·V·O·T

As I plan for a new school year, I hear Ross in my head yelling, "Pivot!" With our ever-changing environment right now, I find myself having to pivot my thinking and expectations often. Just when I think I have my mind wrapped around an idea and start planning, "Pivot!"— changes have been made. In our district, we are beginning the year online. I'm learning a new platform, embracing the components of distance education, learning new procedures, and revamping curriculum. As I do, I remind myself to pivot and think of all the new things I am learning and the new opportunities I have to try something I would not have tried before. There will always be times you are going to have to pivot your expectations and procedures.

As teachers, we need to model our ability to pivot to our students. Our students (and their parents) are watching us and waiting to see how we approach teaching and learning. Our attitude and ability to pivot will directly affect those around us. Involve them in problem solving along the way. Continue to build relationships and show them how we can be successful with this challenge. We have opportunities to be innovative and push ourselves to try things once unknown to us. What an exciting adventure, as long as we can pivot our attitudes to think that way.

Whatever type of teaching model we're going back to this fall, we have to remind ourselves to pivot our actions and attitudes more often. Even though it may not look the way we planned, students will still learn and teachers will still teach. Just keep reminding yourself and your students to "Pivot!"

Melissa McNally

 What speaks to me . . .

Ignite the Spark

You can tell when people are truly happy. Their energy is genuine. — Alexandra Elle

The Tucson Festival of Books is a free community literacy extravaganza celebrating humans and the words they speak and write. When I attended, I was delighted to discover more than 350 authors and presenters sharing literature for children, young adults, adults, and everyone in between. Born out of the desire to improve literacy rates among children and adults in the community, the festival is a family event that has something for everyone.

I think the thousands of participants must have left as I did, with a renewed interest in reading. And, I am wondering how we might keep that exhilarating spirit alive all year. If we continually fuel the fire for ourselves, it will surely translate to our students, their families, and our colleagues, igniting a spark in them that leads to a lifelong love of learning and reading.

With that in mind, here are a few ways we can promote adult literacy in our schools, so the reading lives of teachers and administrators will be healthy and thriving:

- **If you like _____, then you should check out _____.** In the staff room, post a blank piece of chart paper on which everyone is invited to declare what they are reading and recommend other titles.

- **Picture this:** On school picture day, have staff members hold a favorite book. Post the photos outside each classroom door.
- **Book talks:** During team meetings, have each teacher provide a minute-long book talk on what they are reading.
- **Join a reading challenge:** Goodreads has an annual reading challenge. Go to goodreads.com to find out more.
- **Mark it up:** Lend a professional book to a friend and give them permission to mark it up however they wish. Then get together and compare the notes you took and the passages you highlighted. Reflect together on what each of you found most interesting.

If we are rejuvenated, refreshed, excited, and supported in our reading, it is sure to flow over into all we do with children. They won't be able to help it: they'll want to become part of the culture of readers.

Gail Boushey

 What speaks to me . . .

Relationships First

It's the little conversations that build the relationships and make an impact on each student. — Robert John Meehan

"Hi, Samantha. Nice to meet you! My name is Dan. I'd like to start by having you tell me about yourself. I'm looking forward to getting to know you." This was how the photographer of my daughter's senior pictures greeted us when we showed up for her photo shoot on a warm June afternoon. He started the conversation, and then he listened.

He took time to learn about her favorite activities and discover what she wanted to capture in her photos. He lightened the mood by making a few jokes. He asked about her family, friends, school, and work. He even asked her favorite music artists, and played it in the background while they were working. Soon they were talking as if they were old friends, and Samantha was relaxed and at ease as she posed her way through the photo shoot. Dan took time and really focused on the goal: to capture Samantha in this moment and celebrate this stage of her life.

It wasn't the day of her photo shoot that I really appreciated Dan's work; instead it was the day we went to view the images. As soon as I saw them, I understood why he is recognized in his field. He had captured Samantha as the girl we raised and love. He had captured the zest for life her smile radiates, the quick wit and humor behind her laugh, her everyday expressions, and the beautiful spirit we love.

At first, I was surprised at how he was able to get these images, and then I remembered how he had started the session and all the relationship-building techniques he had exercised. His work left me with three observations:

- Conversation—He asked questions and truly listened to the responses.
- Comfortable environment—He outlined the plan, played music of interest, provided choices of settings and poses, and interjected humor.
- Time—He made sure Sam knew she was the focus of the afternoon/evening.

Combined, these observations gave me one giant reminder: relationships must come first. They are the foundation on which excellence is built. When those we work with feel respected and valued, great things happen. This school year, may we take the time to listen to, learn about, and connect with our students and colleagues, building relationships first so learning can follow.

Allison Behne—Photos by McClanahan Studio

 What speaks to me . . .

Accomplish the Extraordinary

We are what we repeatedly do. Excellence, then, is not an act but a habit. — Aristotle

Embarking on a new school year has us planning—creating events, lessons, and moments of learning and fun for the students we are so honored to teach. We hit the ground running with enthusiasm, positivity, and visions of the *extraordinary* dancing in our heads.

As I was thinking about accomplishing the extraordinary, five things come to mind.

1. **Believe in who you are teaching.**
   Be fierce in your belief that all students are capable of learning and deserve uncompromised respect. To accomplish something extraordinary, we must show strength, integrity, and unflagging belief in the children we teach.
2. **Support colleagues.**
   School communities foster learning in students, and the best ones foster learning with adults, too. We must support each other with kind words and respectful actions and by sharing ideas and strategies to create a learning environment that we and our students will be proud to be part of.
3. **Reach out.**
   Building positive relationships with colleagues sets the stage for supporting each other. There are times we need to stretch out a hand for help, and times we need to lend a hand of support.

Developing a culture where help is freely asked for and given builds a strong community and models for students that it is safe for them to do the same.

4. **Read.**

   We know the power of reading for our students. Imagine what would happen if we devoted time each day to our own reading: professional books to challenge our thinking and refine our practice, children's books so we're ready to match students with perfect titles, and fiction or nonfiction of personal interest to broaden our own horizons. Nothing speaks to the importance of being a lifelong reader as loudly as modeling our own love of reading.

5. **Consider one thing you did last year that didn't yield the results you wanted, and give it up or change it.**

   It can be easy to hang on to things that aren't working as well as they should be. This is the year to stare them right in the eye, honestly evaluate their worth, and make necessary changes to bring about success.

Above all, believe in yourself. Find time to reflect, recharge, and remember that you are capable, loving, creative, hardworking, kind, helpful, and amazing. Extraordinary is bound to follow you.

Gail Boushey

 What speaks to me . . .

Empower Yourself

*Eliminate the word **can't** and you'll be amazed at what you can do.* — Billy Cox

When my son first got his PlayStation he was always asking me to play a game with him. My response was "I can't figure out the controllers. If you want to play a game of cards, I will play, but if you want to play PlayStation, ask your dad."

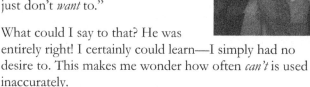

He smiled and said, "I'm a kid and I know how to use the controllers. You *can* learn to play the PS; you just don't *want* to."

What could I say to that? He was entirely right! I certainly could learn—I simply had no desire to. This makes me wonder how often *can't* is used inaccurately.

How often do we hear *I can't?*

- A child: "I can't clean my room by myself."
- A colleague: "I can't get my whole class to grade-level expectations."
- A friend: "I can't lose weight."
- Yourself: "I can't _____."

Have you ever thought about what those words really mean? They indicate that progress has stopped and the speaker has decided there is no solution; they are giving up.

When an individual says, "I can't," do they really mean there is no possible way of doing it? It usually means one of three things:

- I don't *want* to do it.
- I don't *believe* I can do it.
- I don't *know how* to do it.

In all three cases, it is a choice. Replacing *I can't* can be a bit unsettling, because it takes the excuse away and holds us responsible. However, it also empowers us.

Next time you think, *I can't*_____, stop and correct yourself. You can learn if you want to and if you believe in yourself.

Allison Behne

 What speaks to me . . .

Rule Breakers or Rule Makers

I want freedom for the full expression of my personality.
— Mahatma Gandhi

When I gave a direction to a nine-year-old recently, she said, "I'm not breaking the rules. I'm just making new ones." I had two instant reactions: I appreciated the polite yet confident response. And, I just wanted my directions followed. Luckily, this moment was really about a confident kid asserting her desire and it was something minor where I had the option to be flexible.

Classrooms are full of a wide range of personalities. Some of our students are cooperative and quick to follow our directions (bless these kind souls, they help set a tone and support our efforts). However, other students want to be a part of the decision making, want to lead, and want their voices to be heard.

1. Since we are always working to identify students' strengths to build a positive classroom community, we can choose to view the "rule makers" as strong, confident humans willing to make decisions. Giving these students opportunities to shine validates their worth.

2. If we are willing to view the strengths of our "rule makers," we can look for opportunities to allow them to make decisions. One of my students is a great technology problem solver. I have taught him how to pop up, help a peer out, and then get

right back to work. This taps into his strengths and allows him to use them in a positive manner. Likewise, a colleague of mine allows one of her students to share a joke or a funny story once a week during morning meeting. The child gets to have her moment in the sun, but it is only a moment, and the teacher chooses the time and place. When we honor individual personalities, we build healthy, positive relationships.

3. Some things are simply not negotiable. For example, during dismissal, we don't allow students to run into the street. (There is no flexibility when it comes to the possibility of getting hit by a bus!) And, when a child uses a disrespectful tone with a peer, we model different tones to make students aware that *how* something is said is just as important as *what* is said.

We can celebrate individual personalities, creating a time and space for students to contribute to a classroom. Highlighting unique strengths sends the message that everyone in the room is a valuable member of the class community. The work that we put into building a positive community is the solid foundation for all the academic growth we work toward. How can the "rule makers" in your room contribute to your classroom community?

Kristin Ackerman

 What speaks to me . . .

We Must Be Writers

You may not write well every day, but you can always edit a bad page. You can't edit a blank page. — Jodi Picoult

I tend to think of myself as a reader, not a writer. I understand that the more I write, the more confidence I'll gain, and I know I should set aside some time each day to write, yet I easily find other things to do. The busyness I inflict on myself makes the "I just don't have time" excuse much more plausible.

Jen McDonough shifted my thinking at a conference when she addressed the audience:

"Raise your hand if you learned how to teach reading in college." (All the hands went up.)

"And how many of you are readers yourselves?" (All the hands stayed up.)

"Raise your hand if you learned how to teach writing in college, and keep your hand up if you write now." (Only one person raised their hand.)

That was an aha moment for me. Many of us were not taught how to write ourselves, nor were we taught how to teach students to write. It is no wonder we often teach writing with a "do what I say, not what I do" approach. We simply follow a lesson plan that tells students how they should write. Jen said that if we don't experience the joys and struggles of writing ourselves, including writing in the genres and doing the types of writing we are asking of students, we are missing the experiences and background knowledge, and the insights into the ins and outs, that will make the lessons authentic for our students.

The purpose of writing each day became clear to me, and, just as important, so did the underlying reason for my lack of motivation. I truly thought I was missing the writing gene, when in fact I was just missing the purpose of writing, which provides the sense of urgency and motivation. I'd heard that information before, but for some reason, I was in a receptive place to really hear the message this time.

There is an important reason for me to write each day. I must do it if I am to help students from a place of experience. I need to be able to say, "Yes, I too have wrestled with coming up with an idea. Here is what I do when that happens." "Let me show you how I play with lead sentences until I find one I like best." "Let me show you how I sketch out my idea and fill the details in afterward." "Let me show you how I revise when I think I'm finished to make things even better."

I have been able to help students be proficient readers my entire career because I am a reader; I read every single day. Something Jen said has added to this mission: "We are committing ourselves to help this next generation of students be writers, and it is up to us to grow our own writing so we can help them improve their writing as well."

What are you writing today?

Gail Boushey

 What speaks to me . . .

Is Your Mask On?

Self-care is giving the world the best of you, instead of what's left of you. — Katie Reed

Each time a plane departs, directions are given to the passengers on board. We're told where the exits are, that the seat cushions work as flotation devices, and that if oxygen masks appear, we are to take care of ourselves first. The flight attendant says, "If you are traveling with a child or someone who requires assistance, secure your mask first, and then assist the other person."

We take care of ourselves first so that we can help others. That is a powerful concept and one that rings true in many situations. Think of how that rule applies to other professions. A firefighter puts on protective gear and oxygen before entering a burning building to rescue civilians. A doctor or nurse washes their hands before touching a patient in order to prevent further disease. A police officer wears protective clothing, carries necessary tools, and uses communication technology before approaching an unknown vehicle or scene. These protocols are in place for a reason—a person who is hurt or unable to function is not going to be able to help someone who requires assistance. Makes perfect sense.

Now let's look at the teaching profession. Does anyone require assistance from us? Absolutely! Students, parents, and colleagues all need us! So naturally, if we apply the airplane mask rule, we must take care of ourselves first so that we can help others. But this isn't common practice for teachers. We often burn both ends of the candle to make sure our students have everything they need and are getting the most from us. We come in early, work through recess, take a 10-minute lunch, forgo bathroom breaks, and stay after school when necessary. We celebrate the positives, shoulder the negatives, and don't give up— because we believe so strongly in those around us.

That is why it is so important for teachers to join the list of professionals who put the oxygen mask on first. If we do that, we will be better equipped to help our students, and the rewards will be great.

How can we do this when the demands of each day are so intense? We can start by collaborating with colleagues. This provides an outlet for emotions and negates the feeling of being alone, leaving us feeling supported in the work we do. Sharing books, brain breaks, behavior strategies, stress reducers, stories, jokes, tips, hacks, and experiences—all of those will provide us with a breath of fresh air so that we can jump in and help those who need us.

Allison Behne

 What speaks to me . . .

Your Joy

The adventure of life is to learn.
— William Arthur Ward

To me, teaching and learning is magical. It is beautiful and delightful and at times creates a sensation of *how did that just happen?* Witnessing engagement and deep concentration from a teacher and learner as once-hidden information becomes revealed, unfolding a new skill or idea, is pure joy!

The song "Your Joy" by The Coats, a Seattle a cappella group, comes to mind when I see this deep learning. One of the lines is

> I love the sound of a teacher trying . . .

> But most of all I want you to know that I love the sound of your joy.

Teaching and learning is joy! To be on either side of the act is joyful. A college basketball coach once told me he took up guitar lessons during the basketball season. He wanted to play the guitar, and he wanted to be reminded of how it feels to be a learner.

During the school year, we spend most of our time being the teacher. How might we experience the joy of being a learner? Perhaps we'll get acquainted with a new author and read their story, cook a new recipe, learn a new song to sing or play, or discover a new teaching technique.

Once we have learned the skill of teaching it never leaves us, nor does the skill of being a learner. So, in this season, what will you be teaching? What will you be learning? Whatever you do, I wish you joy.

Gail Boushey

 What speaks to me . . .

The Sincerest form of flattery

Imitation is the sincerest form of flattery.
— Charles Caleb Colton

I absolutely love this picture. It's of my uncle Jim, a high school girls' basketball coach, and his granddaughter Georgia. This particular
night was Georgia's fourth birthday, and as honorary team captain, she got to help her "papa" coach. She took this very seriously, watching and copying his every move. When he sat, she sat. When he yelled, she yelled. She intently looked to him for cues about what to do next. It was heartwarming to see her following his example, wanting to be just like him.

A great model can have a tremendous influence on behavior. The same is true in our classrooms.

- The books we bless soon have a lengthy waitlist.

- Our enthusiasm for a new science unit is contagious, and students search for more information and bring it in to share.

- The lessons we demonstrate begin to be internalized and used independently.

- Our respectful dialogue and ability to regulate emotion sets the tone for how we interact.

Modeling provides an example that learners need to be successful. When a behavior, skill, strategy, or concept make sense logically and visually, the learner can more easily enter in and apply the new learning. We see it in how Georgia copycats her papa, and we can use it across all disciplines in our classrooms. Explicit instruction followed by deliberate modeling lays the groundwork for student practice and success. When we are deliberate in our visual, auditory, and kinesthetic modeling with students, we explicitly teach and engage them in a new idea or behavior. We aren't looking for imitation as a form of flattery, but we are hoping to ignite a lifelong love of learning, persistence, and hard work.

Allison Behne

 What speaks to me . . .

Take a Step Back

There is a story behind every person, a reason why they are the way they are. Don't be quick to judge. Be kind and assume the best. — Nicky Gumbel

We did it! "Did what?" you might ask. We finished watching all the Marvel movies in chronological order!

I saw a list posted a couple of weeks back on Facebook, and we took the challenge. Almost every night we sat down at 8:00 p.m. and watched one of the movies as a family.

I had never watched the movies before, but when Avengers: Endgame came out a while back, I thought it was my duty to take my sons, ages 11 and 17, to it because they had seen a lot of the other ones. I asked questions the whole time, and the boys were annoyed. I vowed that I would watch the other movies to get the whole picture, but never had the time . . . Well, now we had the time, so we did it.

Endgame makes so much more sense now! As I was watching it I remembered when I watched it the first time. It was a good movie because of all the special effects, and I enjoyed it because my boys enjoyed it so much, but I didn't understand the why behind anything that was happening. This time around I was invested. I found myself clapping in the middle of it as I got excited about what was happening. I had gotten to know the characters, I knew their backstory, I had gone along for the ride, and now I was cheering them on as they succeeded in their missions, and crying with them in their defeats.

I couldn't help but think how this is true to our real lives. We can see something happen and think, Aww, that's nice or Too bad that is happening, or even judge people for the way they are "going through life." But when we truly know their backstory—things start to take on a different meaning. That is when we can truly cheer when things are going great for someone, and mean it. That is when we can feel the pain for someone as they struggle through the things that life throws at them. When we know each other's stories, we can maybe be a little less quick to judge and a little more apt to lean in and listen. This is true with our colleagues and our students.

So, I wonder . . . whose story do you need to know a little bit better? Who do you need to take a step back from and remember, before you judge, that they too have a story? Who can you be a listening ear for, and who can you invite to tell their story?

And if you have the time and your kids are into the Marvel movies, I highly recommend watching them in order.

Now the question is . . . what do I do with all this time on my hands at night?

Laura Secrist

 What speaks to me . . .

Lasting Affirmations

The most important things in life are the connections you make with others. — Tom Ford

While watching a University of Washington women's basketball game, my granddaughter Hadley drew a birthday picture for her cousin Jenna, her favorite player. After the game, Jenna came over to meet us. She leaned down as Hadley presented the hand-drawn picture and wished her a happy birthday. Jenna gave Hadley a big hug and said she was going to hang the picture in her room. I snapped a couple of pictures and said a few words of congratulations for the win, and Jenna went off to meet with her other fans.

Hadley looked up at me with wide, shining eyes and said, "She is going to hang it in her room."

At that moment, I saw in my mind the many children who have presented me with pictures, handmade gifts, treasures found on the playground, or stories that were dear to their hearts and had to be told. I deeply hope that my response to each offering was as affirming. Seeing the effect of that give-and-take through the eyes of a giver, I was reminded just how powerful a few kind words of affirmation can be.

It takes only a moment to convey— *I see you. I hear you. You are important to me.*

The curriculum we teach, the standards we try to meet—they are all important. But in the busy drive to accomplish so much, let's not forget that it takes only a brief moment to make a connection that will be remembered for a very long time.

Gail Boushey

 What speaks to me . . .

The KonMari Method

Believe what your heart tells you when you ask,
"Does this spark joy?" — Marie Kondo

I recently started watching the Netflix series *Tidying Up With Marie Kondo*. Marie uses what she refers to as the KonMari method to help people declutter their lives. The goal is to cherish everything we have so we can achieve happiness and live comfortably. Believing that a reduced amount of physical clutter results in a happier state of mind, she teaches people to keep only those things that spark joy.

The KonMari method is spreading quickly and is even being transferred to other areas of people's lives. I read that one person went through their list of Facebook friends and questioned, "Does this person bring me joy?" to determine whom to keep and whom to remove. Another person uses it when deciding how to fill her calendar. She asks, "Does this activity bring me joy?" If so, she puts it on her calendar; if not, she doesn't.

The idea of focusing on joy can be used in many situations, but it also reminds me that not all things are joyful and we don't always have a choice. Going to the doctor or dentist or going grocery shopping does not bring me joy, but they are "must-do's" from time to time. And if I look past the event and focus on the outcome, I am able to find joy. For example, if I go to the doctor and dentist, I will keep my body and teeth healthy, which makes me happy. When I go to the grocery store, I have food in my cupboards when it is time to cook a meal and the process is much simpler, which in turn makes me happy. Sometimes the path to joy is not as direct as we might think.

This makes me think about our work in schools. Our outlook can positively or negatively affect our happiness. If we focus on the day-to-day challenges and struggles of teaching, asking if they "spark joy," the answer might be no. However, if we focus on the overarching goal and outcome, asking if teaching and seeing students learn "sparks joy," we will answer with a resounding yes. We are teachers because teaching and children bring us joy, plain and simple. This does not mean *all* aspects of teaching and *all* children bring us joy every moment of every day, but our overall work in this field does bring happiness.

Focusing on joy each day helps redirect our thoughts and change our attitude. Our workday is for students. Without them, we do not have a professional purpose. Looking for the good in each student, cherishing the big and little teaching moments of the day, and finding pleasure in the small things are all steps toward joyful teaching. Create a spark of joy in your teaching, and joyful learning will follow.

Allison Behne

 What speaks to me . . .

Meaningful Mornings

Wake up every morning believing that something wonderful is about to happen. — Brad Tumbull

I was at Issaquah Valley Elementary School in time for a morning staff meeting that was directly on the heels of the previous evening's open house. What a combination— tired upon tired. Standing at the door, greeting each staff member, was the principal, Michelle. As she welcomed each employee, she asked about open house, agreed about being tired, inquired about family members, and listened carefully to the responses, setting the stage for the meeting with the message— *you are welcome, you are important, you are heard.*

As teachers, we can open the door each morning with the same intent, welcoming the line of faces and setting a positive focus. For some, this is the happiest door to be opened. For others walking over the threshold is the beginning of focusing and imagining a positive day to come.

As each child passes, we connect with them. You might even say we take their temperature. We watch to see if anyone's internal thermometer is creating a defense to fight against an infection: How are they feeling right now? Are they ready to learn? We watch for patterns of behavior: this child smiles and locks eyes, the next child's head is down and they're shuffling their feet, this child is yelling in line, pushing their way to the front. A temperature is not an illness; it is just a symptom of the body's response to an illness and is not considered dangerous. What is causing the temperature, and how should it be treated? Can the child resolve the issue on their own or do they need help?

Each child brings a story with them, and in that split-second interaction, we listen and convey that we care about them and love them as a human first. We are opening our class door and offering a world of safety, respect, and strategies for learning today and every day. Even when their internal temperature is radiating distress, we offer them love and strategies to reduce their fever.

The small but mighty act of opening the door and welcoming our students may well be one of the most important things we do all day.

Gail Boushey

 What speaks to me . . .

What Will They Remember?

Sometimes you will never know the value of a moment, until it becomes a memory. — Theodore Seuss Geisel

It happened. I blinked one too many times, and on May 26, my daughter, Samantha, graduated from high school. Beginning on the day she was born, I was

warned how fast the time goes, and now I see why. It seems like yesterday she was standing in the back corner of a stage, crying at her first dance recital, and now here we are, getting ready to send her to college, where she will major in elementary education.

We've spent weeks looking through pictures, viewing video footage from years past, and reminiscing about old times. I found it interesting to hear which events stood out in her mind and about the memories that flooded back to her. As she reminisced, I couldn't help but notice how many times she mentioned school or one of her teachers.

She laughed when she spoke of making pancakes in Mrs. Hellberg's room on the 100th day of school. She smiled when recalling Johnny Appleseed Day, being in a "band" with her friends, high school homecoming, and football games. She shared how nervous she was when she entered a new school as a fifth grader, and how the teachers made her feel so welcome. I learned that her first memory of being made fun of was when peers at her new school didn't understand her desire to wear two different-colored, wild socks. And she shared how special she felt when Mrs. Erickson showed up at her birthday party after Sam invited her to join in the fun.

She burst into song when she remembered the melody Mrs. Flores taught students to help them remember the six pillars of character and told me she will use that same song with her students someday. She teared up as she remembered the day her class was told that one of her dear friends was fighting a brain tumor.

As Sam looked through pictures and shared memories, I thought about how blessed I am to be a teacher. As teachers, we have the ability to make a real difference in the way children perceive the world around them. Our attitudes and responses help shape the way children view and handle many situations, and our words, actions, and emotions are watched closely and felt deeply. When we embrace the blessing and responsibility of being a teacher, we can take comfort in knowing we help shape the future . . . literally.

Years from now our students will look back and remember little things we may not have deemed important at the time. I am filled with gratitude when I consider all the teachers who have made a difference in Sam's life and hope that one day, your names and mine will be spoken with the same kind of tender reflection and regard.

Allison Behne

 What speaks to me . . .

A Better Countdown

Don't count the days, make the days count. — Muhammad Ali

After the winter break it can be tempting to start counting down the days until summer. It is understandable. We are all tired. But I when we start counting down, something happens that isn't in our best interest or the best interest of our students.

I have been thinking about the power of subtle differences. It was in *Choice Words* by Peter Johnston that I learned my students would be better influenced by "Aren't you proud of yourself?" than by "I'm so proud of you." It's a small shift, but the second sentence implies that students work to please me. The first promotes intrinsic satisfaction and self-pride.

So when I saw this sign in the office of Maple Grove Elementary in Waukee, Iowa, I was struck by the subtle difference it's language made. (It says Cherish — You only have 157 days  to make a difference in the lives of others at Maple Grove Elementary. . . where each of our stories matter.) Instead of counting down the days until sunshine and sleeping in, the staff has shifted to an intention to cherish each remaining day and use each one to make a difference. We can do the same.

Whether we are teachers making a difference in the lives of students, coaches making a difference in the lives of teachers, or administrators making decisions that will affect everyone, let's set aside the rituals of counting down and instead, make every single day we have left count.

Lori Sabo

 What speaks to me . . .

Life is Made of Seconds

Today has 86,400 seconds. Use them wisely. — Unknown

I have been chronicling each day of the year by uploading a photo or video to an app that stores the memories. When the year ends, the pictures will be meshed together into my personal year in review. The daily task of choosing an image that represents something from the day is bringing me so much joy. Reflecting on the days before, seeing just that one second of time snapped from that day, has me reliving and remembering other events that surrounded that day as well. Just that one second of time.

Days in our classrooms are filled with moments worth saving. How can we help students remember the special and ordinary events from our year together? Here are three ideas that will help cement memories of a year of learning.

1. Use an App: Download <u>1 Second Everyday</u>: <u>Video Diary</u>, start a classroom account, and take a

video or picture a day. You'll choose which second of the video to keep, and at the end of the year, the program will stitch the memories together for you. Voila! In a matter of seconds you will have a culminating video for your class.

2. Chart the Book: Post a running list of all the books you have read as a whole class. At the end of the year, take a photo or type the list up and send it home with each student. They will treasure the shared memories as they reflect on the titles and journey you did together, and may check their favorites out for summer rereads.

3. A Word a Day: We always end our team meetings with each person sharing a word that exemplifies what they are thinking and feeling. Try this as your students leave for the day. This is a quick way to take the temperature as they leave. You may want to start a list of descriptive words, which they can add to their vocabulary and will help them be more reflective.

These snippets of time captured in pictures and words help us reflect and remember the seconds that add up to minutes, hours, and days in our home lives and in the lives we share with our students. Let's remember them.

Gail Boushey

 What speaks to me . . .

Lessons from the Road

Reflection . . . looking back so the view looking forward is clearer. — Unknown

Recently, my sister and I embarked on a road trip across the Midwest to attend a symposium for teachers. Instead of flying, we chose to hop in the car, turn up the tunes, and enjoy the countryside.

In our 26-hour round trip we uncovered four lessons from the highway that not only benefit us on the road but also at school.

1. **Check your gas gauge often.** While on our drive, we stopped for gas every few hours, because we were well aware of the consequences if we ran out. Teachers should do the same. We must take time to rest and recharge. This can be as simple as a drink of water, a few deep breaths, calming music, conversation with a friend or colleague, or a walk around the school at recess. Ensuring our tank is full will enable us to be at our best for our students.

2. **Detours are just a different way of getting there.** With only 345 miles to go, we came across a detour. This added 10 minutes to the journey, but we enjoyed beautiful scenery as a result. There is always more than one way to get there. The same is true when we teach. No two students are the same, and therefore they often take different paths to learning. Taking a detour or rerouting instruction is a common practice in meeting the needs of our students.

3. **The road is a happier place when drivers use signals.** Whether they're changing lanes, exiting the interstate, or turning a corner, we can prepare better when drivers use their signals. The same is true for our students when we are teaching. When we provide the teaching target, we tell them, "Here is what we are learning today." We provide directions to where we are going so that they can prepare and adjust accordingly.

4. **The company you keep makes a difference.** During the drive, we talked, laughed, shared, and collaborated. Time passed more quickly and certainly more pleasantly. It was especially valuable to have someone by my side who could help with directions. This applies at school, too. Our colleagues are a vital part of our success. Sharing, collaboration, and collegiality are crucial to a healthy work environment.

The number one lesson we learned? When we embark on a journey, the road may be long and filled with turns, hills, and even a few potholes, but if we have gas in the tank, a passenger for company, and a positive attitude, we will reach our desired destination.

Allison Behne

 What speaks to me . . .

Lessons to Learn

Life's best moments usually happen unplanned. — Unknown

Each spring I make lists of things I want to accomplish during the summer break from school: clean out the garage, go through the closets—you know, those all-important tasks that I usually wait all year to do. But now my goals have changed. It took watching our grandchildren, Hadley and Hollis, playing with buckets and balls—dumping them from bucket to bucket, picking up strays, and doing it all over again—to make me think maybe the most  important thing we can do for ourselves and children is to schedule unstructured, nothing-planned time.

With the season of school being so coordinated, and our lives being so scheduled, we quickly find that all of our time is organized and directed, with little time to just "be." Schedule lots of unscheduled time, or nothing-planned time, which is sure to re-energize you for the days to come. And if you need a few ideas of what to do during that time, here is my list:

- Read whatever you want, and lots of it. Novels, professional books, children's books, magazines.

- Watch whatever you have been missing, and lots of it. Movies, TV series, documentaries.

- Talk to whomever you have been missing, and talk a lot.

- Sit and take in the everyday sights around you, and let your mind wander.

We know thoughts of school and improving your teaching craft are never far away. Along with everything else you are doing during the summer or during the year, be sure to fill yourself up with what you like best, whatever that is, and schedule some time to just "be."

Gail Boushey

 What speaks to me . . .

Revising the Recipe

Every student can learn, just not on the same day or in the same way. — George Evans

I love chocolate chip cookies, and over the years I've combined and altered a few recipes to create what I consider the "perfect" chocolate chip cookie. I no longer need the recipe card, because I know how much of each ingredient to add, and in what order, to create the dough. I also know to bake them at 365 degrees for eight minutes. They sit for two minutes to cool before I remove them from the cookie sheet. I have done this for years, and they came out just as I like them every time . . . until recently, when I got a new oven.

I baked the first batch with the new oven just as I always had, and they came out doughy. I put them back in for a few minutes, but they were still not cooked all the way through. I put them in again for a few more minutes, and they came out too crispy. Fail.

So, I tried again . . . Fail. Hmm . . . What was going on? At this point I realized I was going to have to problem-solve, because even though my new oven was very pretty, it did not perform the same as my previous oven. With the next few batches I altered the temperature, baking time, pan, and cooling time, until I was able to find the perfect combination to get the outcome I wanted. Turns out with this oven I need to bake them at 375 for nine minutes and allow them to cool for one minute before removing them from the cookie sheet. Not a huge difference, but enough to make or break the recipe.

If I had not made a few adjustments and instead kept following the recipe to a tee, my cookies would not have turned out as I like them. With the new oven, I had to combine past experience with what I know about baking, and adjust. This is a lesson I can transfer to the classroom quite seamlessly.

Each year we have a classroom of children waiting to learn, and each child is unique. If we take a set of lessons we pulled from a program or used with the previous year's class, or if we try to teach the exact same lessons as our grade-level team, and think we can teach them "as is" and our students will all meet standard and grow, we will quickly find out we are wrong.

It is great to have a place to start, a foundation from which to build, but we need to monitor our students and adjust as necessary so we can teach in the way they learn best. This requires us to look at the materials we use, the instructional strategies we employ, the setting in which we teach, and more. We must use our professional judgment to do what is best for the students in front of us so that they can grow to their highest potential.

Just like we "tweak" recipes in the kitchen to fit our tools and our tastes, we must learn to "tweak" our instructional practices so that they fit our students and their needs.

Allison Behne

 What speaks to me . . .

The Many Meanings of Opportunity

*If you have the opportunity to do amazing things in your life, I
strongly encourage you to invite someone to join you.*
— Simon Sinek

Whenever I begin to write, I open the online thesaurus on
my computer. I'm curious to see the various subtle
nuances in meaning for a particular word I might use. It is

fascinating to see how
two words can be so
close in meaning yet
maintain a slightly
different interpretation.
While updating my class
website, I looked up the
word OPPORTUNITY. When the long list of related words
appeared, my mind began to sort and classify.
Immediately, I could see similar yet distinctive threads
emerge.

Opportunity = Event, Happening, Fling, Occasion

We are a class, a community, and throughout the year we
will have many exciting opportunities for wonderful
experiences.

Opportunity = Moment, Time, Hour, Opening, Space

We have only a set number of months, days, hours,
minutes, and seconds together. We must not waste a bit of
this opportunity.

Opportunity = Stab, Turn, Fair Shake

Everyone has an opportunity to do his or her best.

Opportunity = Hope, Freedom, Connection

Anything is possible when we seize the opportunity to work together.

Opportunity = Good Fortune, Good Luck

If we take full advantage of our opportunities, good things will happen.

It's incredible to see so many facets in 11 letters. It makes Simon Sinek's words about opportunity even more powerful: "If you have the opportunity to do amazing things in your life, I strongly encourage you to invite someone to join you." So, let's do it: let's do amazing things and invite our students along. We'll read, talk, write, hope, share, dream, learn, create, laugh, care, do our best, and build friendships together. What an excellent opportunity for us all.

Trish Prentice

 What speaks to me . . .

When Everybody Wins

Believe you can and you're halfway there.
— Theodore Roosevelt

Two weeks before Tim's 50th state marathon, he fell—twice—on the icy roads of Missoula. The 14 days before a race are usually held sacred for planning and preparation. This time, however, they were filled with therapy, acupuncture, and medication. Still, Tim's back was not healing sufficiently to run a marathon. Normally he would have canceled and rescheduled when his body had recovered, but this race was different.

For the previous two years, 40 people had been planning to travel to the race to watch, cheer, and celebrate Tim's achievement of this 25-year goal. As each person arrived, Becky—his number-one supporter and wife—solemnly reported that her husband might not run. Tim succinctly explained, "I haven't run since the accident two weeks ago."

The day before the event, Tim took his first run with friends and fellow racers to test his ability to compete. That evening, upbeat but cautious, he announced that his body was responding adequately enough to run the race. His goal of finishing the marathon would remain the same.

For runners such as Tim, each race has intermediate goals or objectives. If you believe you can win, of course, you stay focused on what that takes, but other objectives might include such things as running a personal best time or powering through a particularly tough section of the course.

By mile 18 the next day, the injuries that Tim had suffered two weeks prior were having a significant effect, and he questioned whether his body would be able to carry him to the finish line. That is when strategy, mental toughness, years of preparation, and friendship took over. Andy and Eric, two friends who were running alongside Tim, stepped into the important roles of coaching and supporting. Their focus shifted from running their own best times to helping Tim make it across the finish line. Rather than achieving their own personal best times, they ran their most memorable races ever because of their efforts to support their friend. Tim finished the marathon—and all three men were winners.

Currently we are all in what seems like a never-ending race. We struggle to see the finish line, each section of our course seems tough, and we too question if someone is going to need to carry us along the way. However, it is during this race that we have seen teachers, administrators, coaches, consultants, authors, and parents join forces to help each other make it to the finish line. Collaboration is strong, resources are being shared, and we are coming together for our students and each other.

In my opinion, that makes us winners already – even if the finish line has yet to be determined.

Gail Boushey

 What speaks to me . . .

Pick Your Battles

Choose your battles, but don't choose very many.
— Colleen Hoover

You know the condensation that covers a mirror or window when the temperature changes just enough? I remember writing on the windows of the school bus, and similar antics at home, only to be told not to because the windows had just been cleaned. And when my children tried to do the same thing, I always stopped them, too . . . until recently.

A few weeks ago, I went in to tidy up the bathroom after my son's shower and saw a large face drawn in the moisture of the bathroom mirror. My initial reaction was to sigh. As I was about to call his name to remind him that this was not okay, I paused and reflected. In front of me was an adorable drawing that would be completely invisible when the room cleared. Why was it not okay for him to write on the mirror when it was wet? That is when I realized that this harmless act was really not so bad. Then, instead of calling him in, I added to the drawing and wrote him a message.

Since then, we've been taking turns writing back and forth, and I look forward to the messages/art on the bathroom mirror.

I was sharing this story with a colleague when she thanked me for reminding her to pick her battles. She said, "Sometimes I think I have rules just for the sake of it. It is counterproductive to creating independent learners."

Her comment made me think about the classroom and what unnecessary rules could be discarded to enhance a student-centered environment. Maybe if we reduce our need to control all things and focus our energy on important, effective practices, our classrooms won't fall apart as we fear, and instead, maybe our students will reap the benefits. I find it helpful to ask about the purpose of the systems and procedures in place in the classroom. If there is a clear purpose, it is worth keeping. If not, it is time to reconsider. Ask yourself, *why* and *what. Why am I doing this? What are my students gaining from it?*

Letting go of the "no writing on the mirror" rule has led to a new tradition that brings the possibility of surprise with each new day. If such pleasure has come from letting go of something so small, I have to wonder how much joy and surprise might be rekindled in our classrooms by letting our students express themselves more freely.

Allison Behne

 What speaks to me . . .

May I Show You?

The important thing is to never stop questioning.
— Albert Einstein

Pepper, age five, wrote a string of letters across the page, then pointed to them and asked, "Can you read this to me?"

When I responded that the author is the best person to read the work, she replied, "Okay, but could you tell me what it says?"

Instead of decoding BIAVHEYRD, I asked, "May I show you what some writers do when they write a story?" I took another piece of paper, did a sketch, and read my picture. Then I wrote the first sound of each word I had just recited and read her my story, touching each letter as I went. "So, Pepper, when you want to write a story, you can start by drawing a picture and then write about it, using the sounds you know."

Pepper grabbed a colored pencil and drew a square and a large oval on her page. Then she read, "'Mom and Dad are watching TV. Jake and I are watching Mom and Dad.' I need to draw me in a chair, but I can't draw a chair."

"May I show you?" I asked. I modeled a stick chair on my paper. She confidently added one to her own page and drew herself in it. Then she drew another chair and drew her brother in that one.

In no time at all, Pepper had completed her story and learned how to staple a blank sheet of paper on the front for a cover and write "By Pepper" to show she was the author.

As I reflected on this conference later, I thought about the powerful simplicity of asking, "May I show you . . . ?" The question invites us into children's work, gives us a chance to provide precise models, and often instantly moves children forward.

Gail Boushey

What speaks to me . . .

Informed Decisions— Our Responsibility

Make informed decisions, not influenced ones.
— Sneha Acharekar

Our last utility bill provided the confirmation we needed . . . Our windows needed to be replaced. Being a homeowner is a blessing but comes with many responsibilities, one being general upkeep and repairs. Knowing the expense involved, we wanted to make sure we did our homework and could feel good about our purchase.

We asked friends and coworkers, researched internet reviews and consumer reports, and went to a few different retailers before making a final selection. We were surprised to learn that there are many things to consider and many different opinions when it comes to windows. It took some time to sort through all we learned, but in the end, we used the information we'd gathered to make the best decision for us.

Reading and talking with others to gain information is not new. It is a common process when looking for a book or movie recommendation, planning a family vacation, or purchasing a new car. And it is something we, as educators, should do when determining something as important as how and what to teach our students.

When purchasing new windows, it would have been easy to go with the first thing we found, but we would have spent more for lower-quality windows. If we had employed the first retailer we visited, extensive remodeling of one wall would have been necessary, since they didn't have a matching fit. In either scenario, going the easiest route would have ended in extra cost and time wasted.

The same is true in the classroom. Each of us has a unique makeup of students and required standards to teach. If we take the first lesson we see on the internet or adhere to a specific sequence of lessons in a teaching manual, the waste of money and time can be costly. It is up to us to read about, research, discuss, and question instructional practices so that every decision we make is made with the intention, conviction, and knowledge that we are doing what is best for the students in front of us right now.

Becoming a master of our content, and combining that with a deep understanding of our students' strengths and abilities, is what brings deep satisfaction and joy to this profession we love, and purposeful learning to the students we teach.

Allison Behne

 What speaks to me . . .

Introducing Mentors

Every great achiever is inspired by a great mentor.
— Lailah Gifty Akita

I was saddened when I heard of the passing of Katherine Johnson, NASA mathematician, whose calculations aided many critical space missions. She was an accomplished, bright, African American woman who overcame many obstacles on the path toward equality. Katherine's story is told in the book and movie Hidden Figures. Her legacy reminded me of the importance of mentors in our classrooms.

A mentor is generally defined as a close, trusted counselor or guide. Students can develop relationships with mentors to help guide them in particular areas of expertise. Connecting students to expert mentors gives them the opportunity to see how a mentor can help them achieve great things. We tend to think of mentoring as happening face-to-face, but there are additional ways to use mentoring effectively. Let's consider the following options:

Introduce students to a mentor through literature. For example, a student might identify with a character in a book who becomes a role model for them. As a teacher of gifted students, I look to add books to our library with characters who display gifted characteristics, such as the *Max Einstein* series by James Patterson and Chris Grabenstein. I love the book *Because*, by Mo Willems, which tells of the positive effects mentors can have on the lives of others. After listening to this story, it would be fun for students to create their own cause-and-effect story about how a mentor inspired them.

Another option is to use a mentor text to showcase the talents of an author or character. Students and teachers can go back into the text to study and learn from an author for many purposes. This process allows students to see the craft of literature and writing through the lens of an expert mentor. Regardless of the skill level of the students, they can take away something they've learned from that mentor and begin using it in their own work.

When choosing mentors for students, it's important to introduce a diverse group. Find women who excel in mathematics and science. Find mentors who embody diversity in race and gender. It's important for students to see themselves and identify with mentors in order to make text-to-self connections and reflect on their lived experiences. Diverse mentors can help break down barriers and motivate students to achieve.

Mentors pave the way for future leaders, creators, and learners. Using identifiable characters, exemplary text, and the lives of some incredible people can help students reach milestones and be inspired to reach further. Because of Katherine Johnson, many have reached into the beyond. Inspire your students with the best.

Melissa McNally

 What speaks to me . . .

Refining Systems

For every minute spent organizing, an hour is earned.
— Benjamin Franklin

When our daughter was pregnant with our second grandbaby, she invited me over to help her get things

tidied up and organized. Shoes were scattered in different areas of the house, children's artwork was piled on the counter, and untouched mail was stacked by the phone. I thought, *This will be simple—we'll just put everything away.* Which is when we discovered the problem together. Where did everything go? Systems and places were needed to help alleviate the clutter.

I offered a few helpful suggestions, which were met with a pause, a scrunched-up nose, and "That is interesting" which is polite-speak for "That won't work for me at this time." As a coach, I know that great strides are made when I ask questions and really listen to the answers. So I took off my "mom hat" and put on my "coach hat." I asked some thoughtful questions and really listened to the answers. When I summarized the solutions my daughter brainstormed, systems that would really work for her began to take hold.

When systems stall in the classroom, a few questions can

help us articulate a need, discover what is and isn't working well, and refine a practice.

- What am I doing now?
- What is working?
- What is not working?
- What can I design or refine?
- Is this something I can stick with?
- How will I know this is working?

For example, in Lori's second-grade classroom, students would often forget to turn in their homework folders. She decided she needed a system that would elevate the percentage of students who remembered, so she began greeting students at the door every morning with the homework tub in her hands. Each student got a friendly and personal greeting to begin the day, and she got homework turned in before they even entered the classroom.

Whether working to clean up clutter in your room, come up with a new system for turning in completed work, or shortening transition times, these questions can help identify the problem and articulate and implement a solution that will benefit everyone.

Gail Boushey

 What speaks to me . . .

I Love You

They don't care how much you know until they know how much you care. — Theodore Roosevelt

I love you. These three simple words can change attitudes, build confidence, and promote self-worth. And, when believed, change a person's trajectory. I witnessed the power of these words early in my teaching career when a guest teacher spent the day in my classroom while I was out for a training. Andree Halden, a well-known retired kindergarten teacher from our district, accepted the opportunity to work with my students for the day, and I have to admit, I was secretly happy to have a day away.

That year I had 24 students, and the varying needs and personalities mixed with numerous teaching demands were topped with a student who consistently displayed extremely challenging behaviors. It was almost too much. Each morning I gave myself a pep talk about how that day would be different, but within two minutes of this child entering the room, a power struggle ensued. His daily behaviors included throwing his book bag, shouting, taking others' belongings, running, kicking, and frequent bursts of "I hate you!" The class (and I) came to expect his behavior, and even learned strategies for dealing with physical and verbal outbursts. So when I learned I needed to put in for a guest teacher so that I could attend a training, I was more than willing to do so.

I spent ample time preparing to be gone and, in my plans, included a list of strategies Ms. Halden could use when working with the most difficult behaviors. I fully expected to return the next day to a lengthy note from her and a request to be removed from my list of guest teachers.

The opposite was true. I returned to a short note that said the day had been great. The only mention of the student in question was an empathetic comment:

> George had a rough start to the day but nothing we couldn't handle. As soon as I told him I loved him and we would get through it together, things got better. Poor child, he must have a lot going on to be full of such anger. What a sweetie.

I remember the moment I read her note like it was yesterday. "I love you." That is one statement I had never said to George. That is one emotion he had yet to feel from me: love.

I am not going to say that from that moment on, everything was perfect and all challenging behavior ceased, because that certainly isn't true, but I can say that that was the turning point for George, me, and the entire class.

Love has the power to heal, comfort, and unite. It can be life changing.

Allison Behne

 What speaks to me . . .

Our Response Matters

I see you. I hear you. What you say matters.
— Oprah Winfrey

Have you ever texted someone and seen the "read" receipt but not received a response? Or sent a card or gift to someone and wondered if they got it because you didn't hear from them? A lack of reply when we reach out to others can be unsettling. A response, however brief, communicates appreciation and mutual respect.

Our students crave this same attention from us. When they share a story at the beginning of the day or write about an event in a writing notebook, they are sharing a piece of their lives with us. If we are hurried and ask them to tell us later, or don't take time to read the work they share with us, we miss out on a valuable opportunity to connect and confirm that they are seen and heard.

We have good intentions, don't we? Yet when the busy, pressure-filled hum of school life kicks in, we can get side-tracked by other things that feel more urgent.

This fall, when our plates are full and a crowded class of students is counting on us, let's remember what a precious gift being present is.

When we make eye contact and greet each student as they enter, we start the day off with a personal touch. When we read and respond to a few writing notebooks each day, we get to them all in the week, imparting that we value their voice. When we give someone our undivided attention on recess duty, in the bus line, or as we walk down the hall, we communicate their importance to us.

It doesn't take much to focus in, listen intently, and let them know we care. And since we understand the tremendous importance of response in fostering relationships, we know the benefits will be great.

Gail Boushey & Allison Behne

 What speaks to me . . .

Meet Amanda

Your work is going to fill a large part of your life, and the only way to be truly satisfied is to do what you believe is great work. The only way to do great work is to love what you do.
— Steve Jobs

"It's about attitude, relationships, service, atmosphere, and respect." That is what Amanda told us when we asked how she had trained for her position as a bartender and server at the Hyatt Regency in Schaumberg, Illinois. "I love my job. You have to want to do it, and I do. I wait on people the way I want to be waited on."

We stayed at the Hyatt three nights when we were in Schaumberg for our Daily 5/CAFE workshops, and the service we received from Amanda when we went to the hotel restaurant the first night made us return each night afterward. She was friendly,

Doug, Ali, Amanda, Gail, Emily

quickly learning and calling us by name. Knowledgeable, sharing what she knew of the menu. Attentive, knowing almost before we did when we needed something. Humorous, sharing jokes of her own and laughing at ours. And energetic as she served those around her with a contagious smile and kind spirit. We enjoyed getting to know her, and truly believe the feeling was mutual . . .

because that is how she made us feel.

There are many, many restaurants in Schaumburg and the surrounding area, yet Amanda made us want to return to hers. Why? She pegged it in our conversation. It is about attitude, relationships, service, atmosphere, and respect. We think Amanda is on to something, and if we follow her advice in the classroom, our students will want to return each day too.

1. Attitude—Be positive in our words and body language.
2. Relationships—Get to know our students as individuals. What are their interests outside of school? Let them know you care.
3. Service—Make eye contact, at their level, when talking with students. Offer kind gestures when opportunities present themselves.
4. Atmosphere—Create an environment that is inviting, safe, and fun.
5. Respect—Treat our students as we would want to be treated.

Thanks, Amanda, for the great conversation, service, and experience to learn from.

Gail Boushey & Allison Behne

 What speaks to me . . .

Better Than Me

When we seek to discover the best in others, we somehow bring out the best in ourselves. — William Arthur Ward

I live close to the beach and typically run alone early in the morning. However, on Saturdays, most runners drive to the beach road to do their long runs. It is a social event and not uncommon for a stranger running at the same pace as another runner to strike up a conversation.

A few Saturdays ago, I was running on the beach road and ended up running with two other runners. One introduced me to the other by saying, "This is Tom, my better-than-me." He went on to say that Tom was his running partner because Tom is faster and pushes him to be better. As I headed for home, I just couldn't get that phrase out of my head. In life, don't we all benefit when we spend time around people who are better than we are?

In my teaching life, Jen McDonough is my better-than-me. Jen juggles teaching full-time, literacy coaching, two kids, a husband, family, and friends, and yet she is always pushing herself to grow professionally (she even looks cute and put together while doing all of it). Jen is the one I talk to when I want to bounce ideas off someone or need another perspective. She pushes me to try new things, even when they feel uncomfortable. When I have a crazy idea that I'm dying to try, she jumps in to try it in her room too so we can talk about how it worked in K–1 versus grades 3–5.

Teaching can be isolating. Instead of avoiding the better-than-me people in life, perhaps we should run alongside them from now on. Likewise, we should throw our classroom doors and teaching lives open in case we might be someone else's better-than. If we hit our strides together, it can only get better!

Kristin Ackerman

 What speaks to me . . .

Reader's Bonus

WAIT!

We have more to share.
(It wouldn't all fit in this book!)

We wanted to give you each a big hug for all you do
for children every day, but since that was impossible,
we decided to do the next best thing.

It's simple.

1   Go to TheDailyCAFE.com/LightbulbBonus.

2   Let us know who you are so that we can
thank you.

3   Receive your bonus!

Have a Lightbulb Moment to Share?

We'd love to hear it!

Share with us at:
TheDailyCAFE.com/LightbulbMoment.

Who knows, you might just be
in the next edition!

Lightbulb Moments

About the Authors

Gail Boushey is an educator, author, speaker, and entrepreneur. Co-creator of the Daily 5 Framework and the CAFE Literacy System, she is also the co-author of *The Daily 5* and *The CAFE Book,* and co-owner of The Daily CAFE company. She leads a passionate team that equips educators to individualize instruction, increase student independence, and provide authentic work for students.

An innovative teacher, writer, and speaker, **Allison Behne** empowers educators to think outside the box and critically examine their instructional practices by asking, "What is best for my students?" She is the co-author of the expanded second edition of *The CAFE Book* and an Assistant Professor of Education at Upper Iowa University.

Lightbulb Moments

Other Titles by These Authors

The Daily 5, Second Edition: Fostering Literacy Independence in the Elementary Grades

Gail Boushey & Joan Moser

The Daily 5 framework provides a way for any teacher to structure literacy and math time to increase student independence and allow for individualized attention in small groups and one-on-one. One of the most widely read books in education, these practices are based on years of experience in classrooms and brain research.

The CAFE Book, Expanded Second Edition: Engaging All Students in Daily Literacy Assessment and Instruction

Gail Boushey & Allison Behne

The CAFE Literacy System helps teachers apply what research has shown—that reading instruction is not about the setting, the basal, or the book level. Rather, effective reading instruction is based on what that student needs in that moment. CAFE stands for comprehension, accuracy, fluency, and expand vocabulary. The CAFE system helps

teachers organize student information, assess to instruct, make learning visible, and it provides a protocol for teaching lessons in any setting.

These books are available at Stenhouse.com and Amazon.com.

For more information about Daily 5 and CAFE, visit TheDailyCAFE.com.

Made in the USA
Monee, IL
05 December 2020

49544127R10066